Craig

A Man's Guide to Pregnancy

Love,

Sheaa

:)

A Man's Guide to Pregnancy

How to live with a pregnant person and get out of it alive.

by John Zakour

METROPOLIS INK

METROPOLIS INK
USA / Australia

web
www.metropolisink.com

email
inquiries@metropolisink.com

Contents

Introduction 7

What's going on? 8

What to Expect: the First Trimester 9

What to Expect: the Second Trimester 10

What to Expect: the Third Trimester 11

Cravings 13

Talking to your unborn child 14

Preparing a room for the baby 15

Lamaze classes 16

Doctor's visits 17

Little extras to make life easier 18

Things you should NEVER say 20

Things you should say a lot 22

Good things to expect from your wife being pregnant 23

Things you can do to pass the time 24

Selecting the Place of Birth 25

A New Trend 26

FAQs about pregnancy 27

Fears 28

Boy's names 30

Girl's names 31

Baby Showers 33

Common Myths 34

Unbelievable things that you'd better believe 35

The trip to the hospital 36

The Birth!!!!!! 36

Top 10 things to do during the birth 39

The Recently Pregnant Woman 40

Handy Saying Chart 43

Weight Chart 44

Handy definitions 45

Recording what makes your wife happy 50

Recording what displeases your wife 51

Pictorial Records 52

Getting out of trouble 55

Dedication

To my wife and son of course! Without them I wouldn't
have the knowledge or inspiration to write this.

Acknowledgments

To every woman, child, and man who have gone—
or ever will go—through childbirth together.

Introduction

Browsing through bookstores, I noticed that the vast majority of books on pregnancy are heavily slanted to the woman's side (duh). This is all fine and good, and perfectly understandable, but it does take two to make a baby, and most men are at least twice as confused by the whole process as most women. So I decided to help even the odds a bit by writing this book. The purpose of *A Man's Guide to Pregnancy* is to help a man better understand all the changes his pregnant wife is going through. Hopefully, this understanding will make the experience much more enjoyable for all parties involved—thus allowing the man to live longer.

It was also my goal to keep this handy guide short and sweet because, being a man, I realized that most of us have a rather short attention span when it comes to this sort of thing. Plus, to keep it interesting, I tried to use as many sports and remote control references as possible.

Note: To keep from driving myself crazy, I used the word "wife" throughout the book. This was not met to be a moral trip or anything, I just felt it was easier to write the word "wife" all the time then substituting "women who are with child," "mate," "chosen one," or simply "your woman."

What's going on?

Your wife is pregnant. To put it in its simplest terms, she has a real live little **person** growing at a fantastic rate **inside** her **body**.

In the span of roughly nine months this baby will grow from the size of one little cell (really small) to around the size of a watermelon (really big when you think about it—although you might not want to mention that analogy to your wife). In between, hormones fire off, chemicals interact, and this little cell grows arms, legs, organs, and everything else a baby needs to be a living, breathing, little person that will be wrecking the car before you know it.

You're probably thinking: "So, how does this affect me? After all, my wife's the one who does all the work. I just have to sit around and hope the birth doesn't conflict with my tee-off time." But if the truth be known, you actually have the hardest job of all: you have to **live** with a pregnant person!

This means you're living with your own personal Sybil. In other words: sometimes it's as if you're living with Sleeping Beauty, once in a while it will be like you're living with a very horny Madonna, often it will be like you're living with the incredible if-it's-not-moving-eat-it woman, and all too often it will be like living with a scarier version of that girl from *The Exorcist*. You never know who your wife is going to be from one millisecond to another. All you can do is to be ready to apologize at a moment's notice—and duck a lot.

How did this happen?

If you don't know how this happened, consult a medical professional. Or a good lawyer.

What to expect: The First Trimester

The first trimester is a strange time. Your wife may look pretty much like the same woman she was before your sperm and her ovum collided, but her body is going through changes even faster than you can change channels with a brand new remote. Hormones are firing away and all sorts of other chemicals are doing their stuff. The resulting side effects are varied, not only from woman to woman, but for each individual woman from hour to hour.

You can expect that your wife will be more tired than normal. This tiredness ranges from very little, to as if you are living with a female bear in deep hibernation. (A smart husband who plans ahead can also take advantage of this by timing the pregnancy so his wife is in the first trimester during the championships of his favorite sport.)

Another thing you can expect to some degree is morning sickness. The name is kind of general, and with good reason. This sickness can be anything from a little upset tummy to a full-blown, hold nothing back, tossing of one's cookies. Most women fall somewhere in between. The sickness can also appear at any time or throughout the day. So remember, if you see your wife heading towards the bathroom, don't stop her to ask her what's for breakfast—and don't get in her way.

Also, many women have to go to the bathroom more often during

I suppose this isn't a good time to ask what's for breakfast.

9

this trimester. This is another one of those perfectly normal but totally baffling chemical reactions. Once again, if you see your wife rushing quickly towards the bathroom, make sure you stay clear.

Finally, and most scary, you can expect pretty big mood changes. To use the remote control analogy again, she can change her mood faster than you can cycle through all the channels—even if you don't have cable. These mood swings are often directed towards you, the husband, as you are usually the closest object to her, plus you were directly involved with the start of this whole process. Sometimes she'll treat you like you're Fabio or that guy who took his shirt off on that old Coke commercial. Other times she'll treat you like you just gave Fabio a brush cut and made the guy on the Coke commercial put his shirt back on. Or, she may treat you as if you had just shot Fabio, that Coke guy, and her favorite hairdresser. You—being the man—are pretty much helpless here. All you can really do is enjoy the good moods, and batten down the hatches to weather the bad moods. Remember, this probably won't last much longer than a few months.

What to expect:
The Second Trimester

The second trimester is kind of the temporary return to near normal. It's the proverbial calm before the explosion. Your wife will begin to show that she is pregnant but she will act pretty much like a larger version of the woman you married. If there's anything you and your wife ever wanted to do but haven't had the chance, this is the time to do it. After this trimester, your wife is first going to be too pregnant to move a whole lot, and then you're going to be married with child and you'll both be too worn out to do a whole lot.

One cool thing does occur in the second trimester: you can actually feel your baby inside your wife. The baby makes its presence known through kicking—presumably in some form of Morse code that only babies can understand. While the kicking might be a slight annoyance to the mom, it will be the ultimate in coolness to you—sort of like the feeling you'd get if you could watch four football games and the Playboy channel at the same time. This will probably be the first time when you actually realize that, "Yes, there is a living, growing, little future Hall of Famer inside of there." The only downside of kicking is that it usually occurs (or is more noticeable) at night, thus preventing your wife from sleeping. Which means that if you have an inconsiderate wife she may wake you up, figuring if she's up then you're up. Just think of this as practice for your child's teenage years when he'll really be keeping you up late at night.

The second trimester is also the time that many expecting mothers will undergo ultrasound. Ultrasound is taking pictures with sound waves. The procedure is totally painless for both the father and the mother—and the baby. It's what doctors use in order to: determine the sex of the baby, make sure everything is progressing okay, and have something extra to charge you for. At the end of the procedure they will present you with the first picture (though you'll have to pretty much take the word of the medical professionals that this really is your child) of your unborn child. If it still hasn't sunk in yet, it will now—you're going to be a father. Oh, at this stage don't worry if the baby doesn't look like you—because it won't. This is nothing to be alarmed about and no reason to consult a lawyer. At this stage all babies look pretty much like small versions of those aliens from *Close Encounters of the Third Kind*.

To sum it all up: the second trimester is pretty cool.

What to expect: The Third Trimester

You've heard the saying: *Hell has no fury like a woman scorned*. Well, that saying should be: *Hell has no fury like a woman scorned who's in her third trimester*.

Remember the first trimester? The third trimester brings more of the same—only worse. Now you'll be dealing with a bigger, more apprehensive, more easily riled version of your wife. (Though at times this woman will not seem at all like the woman you married.)

First off, sitting down will be an effort for her and something that is impossible to do gracefully. Never—ever—laugh, or even snicker at her while she is attempting to sit. If you do (despite the fact that standing up is even harder than sitting down) she'll be on top of you faster than a hungry leopard on a blind, wounded deer. Your best plan of action here is to always keep a straight face (if you have trouble doing this, just remind yourself how much your hospital bill is going to be) and offer to help ease her down and help her up. This will not only help your standings with her, but it also builds your biceps and back muscles.

Second, by now the baby is sitting on her bladder. So, remember those sprints to the bathroom during the first trimester? Now they're back, only more so—plus to make matters even worse, now it's hard for your wife to do anything more than waddle. Still, it is amazing how fast a pregnant woman can waddle when nature calls, and calls— and calls. Once again, be prepared to get out of the way fast or you'll end up as road kill.

Finally, all this adds up to one large and angry woman. Rabid attack dogs have been known to cower in fear of women in their third trimester. The slightest thing could set her off. Whatever you do, do not laugh at her waddle—especially if she's on the way to the bathroom (in some states this is considered grounds for her to legally kill you). You should be on your best behavior or you'll run a very serious risk of your child growing up without a father. Just pretend you're one of those guys on the bomb squad deactivating a really sensitive, really deadly, explosive that will explode in your face if you even look at it funny. In order to survive you have to be as quiet and as cautious around it as possible.

Now that she's in her third trimester Gloria always
takes the shortest route to the bathroom.

Cravings

Honey, I know you're eating for two now, but do you really need to carry that around?

Cravings are extreme longings for a strange food or strange combinations of food that can appear at any time during pregnancy. In theory, these cravings can occur any time during a pregnancy; in reality, these cravings always occur in the dead of night on the coldest day of the year (even during the summertime). These cravings can vary from things like a peanut butter sandwich with pickles, olives, and catsup, to really disgusting things such as Spam and airline food.

Cravings are very easy to deal with. Simply do everything in your power to satisfy them—even if this means making a quick road trip to Siberia for really natural frozen ice cream. It is worth it for the peace of mind and the quiet you will receive for making your wife happy (and remember, she can't hit you while you're gone).

Talking to your unborn child

It's nice you are talking to the baby, but do you really need to show him the remote...

Believe it or not, your wife is probably going to insist that you talk to or even read a book to your *unborn* child. This is because a number of studies done by scientists (who were obviously really bored) seem to have shown that talking to an unborn child may be embarrassing for you but good for the baby. It's one of those theories like "No two snowflakes are alike." They can't prove it, but you can't disprove it either. Since they are scientists (who for some unknown reason specialize in this sort of thing) and you're not, guess who your wife is going to listen to?

Your best course of action is to grin and bear it, and hope nobody is watching you on a hidden camera or something. It will help you get through this if you talk about subjects that are near and dear to your heart, such as your favorite TV shows and sports teams. This will allow you to keep at least some semblance of your manhood. Plus, if those wacky scientists are right, your baby will be born with incredible taste. Of course, the best benefit from all this will be you'll get a happy wife, and a happy pregnant woman is much easier to deal with than a non-happy one.

Preparing a room for the baby

Before you bring a baby home, it would be an especially good idea if you have a place ready for it to stay. This is something that should be done sooner rather than later. For example, it's nearly impossible to put up ducky wallpaper while your wife is complaining that her water just broke. And, it's totally impossible to assemble a crib while rushing a pregnant woman to the hospital.

You might think you'll have time to prepare a room while your wife is in the hospital recovering, but trust me, you won't. After the baby is born you'll be too upset thinking about the medical bills and about having to change diapers to do much of anything that requires the use of tools. So, start early—sometime in the second trimester (when your wife is at least near normal) is probably best.

Preparing the baby's room is actually quite easy and far less trying then dealing with a pregnant woman. In fact, it is probably something you may want to do from time to time just to get a break from your wife. Just remember that babies are very simple people. They basically just look around, poop, eat, spit, cry, poop, eat, spit, and cry. Therefore they really don't need a lot of excess stuff in the room. Just make sure you have a nice safe bed and some cool things for them to look

Yes, it's great that the crib is almost ready, but my water broke over an hour ago...

15

at. Unfortunately though, no matter how many footballs you place in the room, the baby is not going to think of these as anything other than something else to spit up on.

Lamaze classes

Lamaze classes are interesting—mainly to women. Here is where you and your wife go to learn how to do something that humans have been doing for millions of years without classes. That is, until somebody somewhere figured out, "Hey, we could teach people to have a baby the natural (more painful) way and charge them for it." Once again, your wife is the one who's having the baby, so the class pretty much centers around her.

Your main duties are to say, "breathe" and to massage your wife in numerous places that you probably wouldn't normally think of, while also trying to look concerned and macho at the same time. Therefore, your goals at Lamaze class will be: staying awake, and trying to look like you're paying attention.

Looking like you're paying attention is easy; you probably had a lot of practice with this when you were in grade school. Just nod your head a lot and mumble things like, "Interesting," and "Wow."

Staying awake is a little trickier, because, as I said earlier, you don't have a lot to do here. My secret to staying awake: keep your mind busy by playing mental games. A couple of the games I liked to play were: checking for husbands that look more confused than me, and trying to guess whose wife had gained the most weight. If this doesn't

The thing I learned in Lamaze class is to never tell your wife that the Lamaze teacher is cute...

work, there's another sure-fire technique you can use: visualization. Sometime near the beginning of the first class the instructor shows a tape of an actual, live woman giving birth to an actual, live baby. This scene—while being wonderful and beautiful and all—is just as gross as anything you'll see watching say, *The Terminator*, and <u>really</u> scary since this is real. So whenever you feel yourself dozing off just visualize an actual baby bursting out of your wife while you watch. This will pretty much jolt you awake for a while.

Doctor's visits

The closer you get to the actual birth the more you and your wife will have to go to the doctor. This is so you know everything is going along okay, and so the doctor can keep making those payments on the Porsche.

While these visits aren't easy on your wallet, and can be a bit painful for your wife and probably even a little gross for the doctor, they are usually pretty painless for you. As long as you don't look in the wrong direction at the wrong time, these visits can be a good chance for you to catch up on some magazine reading—and they're a darn good reason for missing some work.

The hardest thing about being an ob/gyn is learning not to say, "oh gross," a lot...

Little extras to make life easier

There are a number of things you, the husband, can do to make the pregnancy more enjoyable for the wife, and therefore less dangerous for you. The following is a handy list of suggestions. Feel free to improvise on this list—just be careful.

1) Let her use the remote once or twice. If you are feeling extra generous you could even let her watch what she wants to watch now and then.

2) Pick your own socks and underwear up off the floor at least once every other day.

3) Take her out to dinner at a restaurant that doesn't employ people with paper hats or require its customers to carry their own trays. If, due to budget constraints, you must take her to one of these restaurants, at least carry her tray for her.

4) At least pretend to listen when she talks to you. Remember to use phrases like: "Yes, dear," "Of course, honey," and "I don't deserve you."

5) Take her to a movie that doesn't have a car chase or multiple mutilations. (Remember, it's not such a hot idea to take her to any movie that has hacking and slashing off of body parts. This is not something you want a pregnant woman thinking about—she might get ideas.) If you want to be especially nice, take her to a foreign movie with subtitles—she'll enjoy it, and it will give you a good chance to catch up on some sleep.

6) Give her a massage. It will make her feel better and then she'll owe you one. (Remember, though, you don't want to be walking on her back—and you certainly don't want her walking on your back.)

7) Bring her a "thinking of you" present now and then. Note: a bowling ball isn't a good "thinking of you" present—especially if it's drilled to match <u>your</u> hand.

8) Make sure she knows—no matter how big she actually is—that you think she is NOT FAT. Just keep repeating this phrase over and over until you can say it with a straight face. "No, honey, you are not fat; you have never looked better!" Those simple words can save your life.

I see you forgot to lower the seat again.

9) **Most Important**: Don't forget to lower the "seat". There are few sights worse than seeing a pregnant woman stuck in a toilet, and there are few things more dangerous than a pregnant woman who has just become unstuck from a toilet.

Things you should NEVER say

Pregnant or not you still only get one vote in family meetings.

The following is a list of things you should never even consider or think about saying to your wife—or any other pregnant woman for that matter.

1) "Boy, you're fat." This will get you pretty much killed. (See above.)

2) "Have you seen my *Sports Illustrated* swimsuit issue?" Not a good idea—especially if your wife has access to a shredder.

3) "Don't interrupt! The game is on!" This is an especially bad idea if your wife has been mentioning things like, "These contractions are really close together!" or "I think my water just broke."

4) "I'm going out with the guys. I'll see you next week sometime." If you say this, chances are you won't live that long.

5) "Damn, woman! Your feet look like they should be attached to an extra large elephant!" You'll feel like you got run over by an extra large elephant if you utter that.

6) "I'm sure those labor pains aren't nearly as painful as my old football injuries." She'll probably jam a football into some part of your body.

7) "Your doctor's nurse sure is hot!" or (if she's a female), "Your doctor sure is hot." You should only say this if you feel like having your wife change doctors or stop making you come to her doctor's visits. (Remember, by saying this you also run the risk of needing a doctor afterwards yourself.)

8) "Oh, by the way, the guys are coming over tonight for some poker." She's bound to poke you.

9) "My mom's right, you are a bitch." Enough said.

Dear, the Winslows would like you to please
stop scaring their pit bulls...

Things you should say a lot

1) "The bigger you get the more I love you."

2) "Yes, dear, you'll make a great mom."

3) "I find pregnant women (that I'm married to) very sexy!"

4) "Yes, dear, you will return to your normal size."

5) "If it's a girl I want her to be just like you!"

6) "You look radiant today!"

7) "Can I make (or order) dinner tonight?"

8) "Why don't you invite your mom over for a while?" (Okay, this one can lead to a big sacrifice, but it will be worth it in the long run.)

Good things to expect from your wife being pregnant

Not everything about your wife's pregnancy is hard on you. The following is a list of some of the benefits you will receive from your wife being pregnant.

Forget about it stud. When the baby comes the breasts go.

1) Her breasts are going to grow.

2) You'll soon have another tax write-off.

3) The two of you can board airplanes early.

4) She'll sleep more.

5) Your mother-in-law will probably like you better—at least for a day or two.

6) You can buy a bunch of cool toys and tell people they're for the baby.

7) You can show your buddies what a stud you are.

8) If you accompany your wife to prenatal checkups you can miss some work.

9) She will be horny now and then.

Things you can do to pass the time

As your wife grows and grows there will be less and less she will be able (or at least willing) to do. Still, it is possible for you to do many activities together. This can actually be a nice bonding time.

1) Pick out names for the baby (see lists included in this book).

2) If you are religious you can choose the godparents. Even if you aren't religious it can still be a fun—or at the very least an interesting activity—trying to decide who you want to be "backup" parents.

3) Work on the baby's room. This gives you a good chance to play with your tools and stuff. (Notes on this also included in book.)

4) Go for long walks together. (Note that by the third trimester a long walk should never take your wife too far from a bathroom.)

5) Play cards together. (Note: she probably won't be in the mood for strip poker, but you never know.)

6) Watch those videos and DVDs you've always wanted to rent but never had time. Now's your chance, as once the baby comes you certainly won't have time.

7) Have a nice romantic dinner, just the two of you. This is something you'll really look back on and appreciate after the baby is born.

It's great that you remembered to phone the doctor and grab your wife's insurance card and bag. Now if you had just remembered her...

Selecting the Place of Birth

Back in the old days (before the 1990s) people didn't really have lots of choices where their baby was born. It was pretty much understood that you would have your baby at the hospital that delivered babies that was closest to where you lived. This made perfect sense. If you can help it, you don't want to be driving too far with a woman in labor.

Of course this was all before hospitals and birthing centers figured they could make more money by fighting over your insurance money. Today's expecting parents have far more options than our ancestors. Nowadays, area hospitals have special birthing centers and they advertise and compete for your (and your wife's) business. They all offer different luxuries and perks for having your "birthing experience" with them. Some of these include: having your loved ones in the room with you, having your baby in water, having special music pumped in—the list goes on.

This is a very personal choice between a woman, her husband, their insurance company and their accountant. I would never suggest which option is best. Just remember, when a woman's water breaks you really want to be in the hospital as it is not only a bit unnerving, it can also be very damaging to your car's leather seats. Plus, no matter what a woman says about wanting to be surrounded by her loved ones, when push comes to shove (literally here) she's not going to give a darn who's in the room besides the doctor and nurses (as they are the ones who can give her the drugs.)

Another option that has been gaining in popularity is having your baby at home with the aid of a midwife. I'm sure this is a perfectly safe option, as many midwives deliver as many babies in a year as many doctors. Plus licensed midwifes are backed by doctors and hospitals just in case there is an emergency that needs extra care. Still, I may be an old-fashioned guy, but having a baby at home is a bit too old-fashioned for my tastes. There are times when having a highly trained hospital staff and modern drugs around are good—if not for your wife's comfort than at least for your comfort.

A New Trend

One of the newer trends that has been popping up lately has been "baby's first picture." These pictures are taken in the mall with 3D ultrasound. They give you a much clearer picture of your baby than standard ultrasound that most hospitals still employ.

A couple of questions are worth asking here. The first, do you really need a picture of your baby while he or she is in the womb? Chances are you are going to be taking lots of pictures of your baby at more appropriate times, such as when he or she is out of the womb. Chances are you are going to have lots and lots of pictures of this child. Pictures are great because they help you recall happy memories. (These pictures will be used a lot once your child becomes a teenager and starts talking back, wanting to borrow the car and being oh-so-certain that you know nothing.) These pictures will also be much easier to take and less expensive than in-womb pictures.

Also, you should probably ask yourself if it is worth it to bombard your unborn child with extra sound waves just so you can get a snapshot of them. True, there is always the chance that these extra waves may cause your child to develop super powers like the Hulk or Spiderman, but you have to realize the chances of this happening are very very remote. While the procedure is probably quite safe, it can't be safer than not doing it.

I for one would be a bit leery about using a mix of mall photography and medical science. I'm just picky like that.

FAQs about pregnancy

Here are some of the most frequently asked questions about pregnancy.

What will the newborn look like?
A dirty, wrinkled prune with arms and legs that makes a lot of noise. Not nearly as clean and pretty as they look on TV.

Can my wife and I still have sex?
Sure, for most pregnant woman sex is okay until well into the third trimester. Consult with your doctor for exact advice—they love talking about things like this.

Will my wife want to have sex after the baby?
Yes—eventually. Of course finding time might be the trick. You will have to learn to be very efficient.

How exact is this due date thing?
(*In other words: Can I play golf on my wife's due date?*)
Due date calculation is not a very exact science; it is usually plus or minus two weeks, and this also depends on the woman and the number of children she has had previously. A good rule of thumb is to find out when your wife's doctor will be on vacation as this will probably be when she has the baby.

Are pregnant women dangerous?
Usually, no. They can be moody though, so you just need to remember this simple rule: Do whatever they tell you to do

How big will my wife get?
It differs for all women. Some women gain twice the baby's weight, others gain more. A word of advice: don't ever say anything about this.

Fears

Even though you are a strong, macho kind of guy, it is still natural that you will have fears about your wife's pregnancy—pretty much everybody does. Here are some of the more common fears; these are from a study done by Shapiro (1987). These are included just so you know you are not alone.

Queasiness
This is probably the most universal fear. Most men believe they are macho and tough, and that they're not supposed to get queasy. They are wrong. Pretty much everybody gets queasy now and then when dealing with this. Just take a few deep breaths; you'll live. Even if you do pass out during delivery, you'll probably be surrounded by medical professionals, so after they deliver your baby they'll help you. Think of it this way: if you're going to pass out, there's no better place to do it. And don't worry about your wife; she'll be so busy giving birth she won't even notice you're gone.

Increased responsibility
Many men worry about this one so much they take on an extra job to help feed the extra mouth. When dealing with this fear, remember what the late Senator Paul Tsongas once said: "No man on his death bed ever said, 'I wish I had spent more time at work…'"

Loss of spouse and/or child
Almost every expectant father mentions this one. They are afraid that something will happen to their wife during birth. Obviously this is a real fear, but luckily with today's modern techniques most births are quite safe. Heck, people had babies for millions of years before things like hospitals and antibiotics, and most of them came out just fine. If you're religious, a little praying can't hurt. Even if you're not religious, a little prayer can't hurt—you might become religious during the birth.

Feeling vulnerable
We live in crazy times; the divorce rate is now almost as high as the marriage rate. Some new fathers worry that their marriage won't be able to take the added stress of adding a new person to the family

mix. This is a normal concern, but humans are often much more flexible and adaptive than we give ourselves credit for. You and your wife need to be open and flexible. It takes a little work, but adding a child to a family can be a really cool thing. (You get to play with cool toys again and nobody looks at you all funny-like.)

Feeling abandoned

Some new fathers feel abandoned during pregnancy and try to make up for this feeling by having an affair. Note to these fathers: feeling abandoned is normal and will pass. Soon your wife will remember that you exist again. Try to find other safer, more productive, ways to spend your free time than by having an affair. Try golf.

Boy's names

Remember, the name you give your son is the name he'll have to live with for the rest of his life—or until he grows old enough to hire a lawyer to legally change it.

Acceptable boy's names
The following is a list of names that you could give a boy and be reasonably certain other kids won't make any more fun of him than normal.

Robert

Charlie

John

Paul

George

(Nope, Ringo is out)

Mark

Matt

Andy

Luke

Steven

Ken

Christopher

Mike

Tom

Bo

Brad

Zach

**I don't care how popular he would be.
We're not naming the baby Nintendo.**

Boy's names to avoid

Giving a boy one of these names is the same as stamping "beat me up a lot" on their forehead.

Maurice

Melvin

Marvin

Homer

Elvis (There was only one king)

Girl's names

Acceptable girl's names

The following is a list of girl's name that you can use without having other people say: "Huh?"

Carol

Caroline

Cathy (with a C)

Cindy

Dawn

Debra

Jessica

Lisa

Madonna (Just making sure you're paying attention)

Margaret

Marie

Mary

Melody

Nancy

Natalia

Natalie

Olga (It's my wife's name—I have to include it)

Rachel

Rebecca

Sally

Susan

Teri

Girl's names to avoid

These names will either make guys think your daughter is easy, or cause her to sue you—or both.

Flower

Zelda (Cool video game, lousy name)

Snow

Rain

(Any other weather condition)

Bunny

Baby Showers

Baby showers have traditionally served two purposes. They have been a way for women to get together to shower the mom-to-be with presents (get it) and advice on how to rise their baby. Second and perhaps more importantly, they also gave the expectant mom some time with her girl friends and girl relatives so she could vent her frustrations on how her husband (you) aren't caring and loving enough.

This is all fine and good, and since these things are traditionally held on Saturday or Sunday, that means you get some much needed free time to catch up on your sports watching. It also means not only do you get some cool, free stuff for your kid (and you) to play with, but your wife will also be much more relaxed. This relaxation is twofold, due to the sharing of ideas with others and her venting to her friends. Venting to her friends is much better than her venting to (on) you. Not only don't you have to listen, but she'll be pleased to learn that her friends' husbands were just as big of bozos as you are. This will make her happy. No woman wants her husband to be special when it comes to this sort of thing. So traditional showers are good things.

There is catch though; a few years ago somebody somewhere thought it might be fun (for some strange reason) to have co-ed showers. That means not only do you miss your sports events, but your wife misses her venting. This is not a good thing. Not only that, but you may have to partake in all sorts of very unmanly types of games often played at these types of events.

Luckily, there are a few things you can do to make the day still work for you (and your wife). One of them is to seek out the other guys there. This could be a good opportunity for you to practice your male bonding skills. After all, any place that has a party must also have a TV and refreshments. Seek these out with your fellow men. Heck, we used to be hunters and gatherers, so there is no reason why we can't do it again. This not only allows you to talk about sports and to complain about your wives, but with you and the other men out of earshot your wife and her friends (and relatives) can bond and vent (though women usually don't need much of a reason to bond).

The other thing you can do is take bathroom breaks. Nobody

ever questions when a man needs to use the bathroom. Even if somebody does have the gall to question you, you can cut it short with these two simple words, "Bladder infection." If you time these right you can miss all and any silly games or activities.

With a little work (and a little luck) you can make the co-ed shower, if not a win/win situation, at least something you can tolerate for an hour or three.

Common Myths

Myth #1: All taxi drivers are trained to deliver babies.

Truth: Most taxi drivers aren't even trained to drive or speak English!

Myth #2: The more pregnant a woman gets, the hornier she gets.

Truth: Think about it. If you had something inside of you that was stretching your body to new proportions, causing you to retain water, and forcing you to drag around a bowling ball all day, would you be eager to relive the process that caused this?

Myth #3: An angry pregnant woman can beat up 10 trained commandos.

Truth: An angry pregnant woman can beat up 11 trained commandos.

Myth #4: Riding a tractor can cause a woman late in her third trimester to go into labor.

Truth: Women in their third trimester don't ride tractors.

Unbelievable things that you'd better believe

1) Your wife's feet are going to grow to roughly the size of an elephant's.

2) No matter how well you plan, you're going to forget a whole bunch of things.

3) A human being the size of a small watermelon is going to burst out of a spot the size of walnut.

4) You're going to talk to a stomach.

5) Everybody you meet is going to know more about being pregnant than you.

The trip to the hospital

No use writing much about the trip to the hospital, because you won't even remember it. One minute you'll be at home watching the game on TV, relaxing and minding your own business. Suddenly, your wife will tell you, "It's time." First you'll say, "Time for what?" Then it will hit you. The next thing you know you'll be at the hospital timing how long it is between your wife's contractions (screams of pain) while trying to catch the end of the game.

The Birth!!!!!!

The birth of your child will be one of the toughest ordeals you will ever face in your life. This isn't because the birth is actually tough on you or anything, it's because the pre-birth—the labor pains—are painful on your wife so she's going to take it out on you.

For the first two to twenty-two hours of your stay in the hospital you are going to be pretty much alone in a room with this large angry woman in great pain that she blames you for. Nurses and maybe even a doctor or two will check in to make sure all is progressing well and that she hasn't killed you, but until she gets sufficiently dilated (see definitions below) there's not much else they can do. Your main goal here is to survive by keeping your wife as close to happy as humanly possible. This is no small or simple task. Your wife is in pain, and probably a little nervous that now she's going to have somebody else to pick up after besides you.

During this stage, your first instincts will be to run and flee—but you're going to have to fight those instincts. Just remember: if our cavemen ancestors could survive dealing with pregnant cavewomen, then surely you—modern man—can survive dealing with a modern pregnant woman. After all, you have relaxation techniques and painkillers to rely on that your cave ancestors could only dream of. Just try to keep your wife calm and happy by holding her hand and saying nice things like:

1) "Don't worry, dear. I'm sure this will all be over soon and we'll have a nice new baby to raise."

2) "Yes, dear, I'm scum. I don't deserve you."

3) "Nurse, I think my wife needs more painkillers."

Ah, when I say "Push," I mean the baby, not
your husband...

4) "Yes, dear, I'm scum. I don't deserve you."

5) "Nurse, I think I need more painkillers."

6) "Yes, dear, I'm scum. I don't deserve you."

7) "I think the nurses are very nice."

8) "Yes, dear, I'm scum. I don't deserve you."

9) "The hospital has a nice magazine collection."

10) "Yes, dear, I'm scum. I don't deserve you."

11) "This magazine has a very interesting article about
Tom Cruise and Cindy Crawford in it."

12) "Yes, dear, I'm scum. I don't deserve you."

13) "You want to cut what off?"

14) "Yes, dear, I'm scum. I don't deserve you."

15) "I love what they've done with this wing
of the hospital."

16) "Yes, dear, I'm scum. I don't deserve you."

17) "I think you're supposed to breathe more
and curse less."

18) "Yes, dear, I'm scum. I don't deserve you."

19) "No, dear. You really don't want to cut that off me..."

Finally, after an amount of time that seems at least ten times as long as it really was, your wife will be pretty much dilated and all tuckered out, which means the doctors and nurses will roll her into a delivery room as now she's safe to deal with. This part of the birth will be the exact opposite of the first. There will be plenty of people around to help you and it will go faster than you can believe.

There are two rules for you to follow here:

1) don't get in the way, and

2) don't look anywhere you shouldn't.

If you follow these two simple rules you'll be a spit-covered father way before you know it.

Trust me, it may seem like it, but you're really not 18 months pregnant...

Top 10 things to do during the birth

This is handy top 10 list for you to remember what to do while your baby is being born. You can use this as a reference card.

10) Wipe your wife's brow. Believe it or not, having a baby is quite a workout and she'll work up a little sweat.

9) Keep saying helpful phrases like: "You can do it."
"Push when the doctor tells you too."
"I hope the baby looks just like you."
"Doctor, you do accept our insurance. Right?"

8) Tell a joke. If your wife doesn't kill you it will help ease the tension.

7) Just shake your head and agree when your wife threatens to hurt you because of what "you did to me." Most wives hardly ever follow up on these threats.

6) Keep looking your wife in the eyes—eye contact is reassuring and not nearly as icky as looking lower.

5) Start planning on what you'll be buying for Mother's day.

4) Remember, while it's certainly okay to help your wife scratch, you shouldn't scratch yourself where you usually scratch yourself.

3) Tell your wife you love her.

2) Try to remember those breathing exercises they taught in Lamaze class and have your wife do them.

1) Don't forget to keep breathing yourself. You'll be surprised how much easier the pregnancy will be for all involved if you don't faint.

The Recently Pregnant Woman

This book would be incomplete if it didn't at least mention how to deal with "the recently pregnant woman." After all, this woman isn't much different than the pregnant woman, she's just shrinking instead of expanding. This woman may even be a bit more easily aggravated as she is sleeping less due to the fact there is now a crying baby in the house. Make no mistake about it, for the first month or two (which will seem much longer) the baby will pretty much do nothing but eat, poop, cry and sleep, and not necessarily in that order.

Some of your wife's hormone levels are dropping, and others are rising. So, she will be on an emotional roller coaster (yes, again). Therefore, this can also be a hard time for you. You have to accept the fact that you have fallen down your wife's list of priorities in life. Besides you, she now has this baby to take care of. As one of my friends so eloquently put it right after his wife had their first baby, "I've lost her. All she sees is the baby now."

Believe it or not, this is because the baby is even more helpless than you are. The baby can't use the remote or microwave or anything. Plus the baby has the advantages of being cuter than you and of having spent nine months inside of your wife building some sort of mother/child bond. So, there's not much you can do about this. There are a few things to remember here though.

First off, don't look at it as losing a wife, think of it as gaining a child. Remember, children have all sorts of benefits:

They make good tax breaks.

They are fun to play with.

They give your wife somebody else to get mad at besides you.

They make you feel extra manly knowing you are passing half your genes onto the future.

When they get a bit older they will think you are perfect no matter how much of a screwup you are. They give you this priceless kind of unconditional love that is even more special than that you get from your dog. It's true. (Of course this will get balanced out in the future when no matter what you do they will think you are a total jerk. But that's the topic of another book.)

Second off, there are things you can do to help your wife and child:

Learn to change diapers. Modern diapers are pretty much a snap to take off and put on. Plus, if your baby is breast-feeding they (the diapers) don't even stink. Believe me, changing a diaper is a great

Now that I'm not breast-feeding, I'm not sure what I appreciate more: coffee or my husband being able to do the late night feedings...

way to help out, without really going too far out of your way.

Give your wife a break now and then. Take the baby for a stroll. It is very possible for an ambitious dad to walk a child without the mother being around.

Keep using positive reinforcement on your wife. Say handy things like: "You're doing a great job." "She looks just like you!," and "Soon he'll be off to college and we'll miss these times."

You should encourage your wife to breast-feed. There are all sorts of studies showing how this is beneficial to both the woman and the baby. Breast-feeding will have a calming affect on everybody involved: the baby, your wife and you. Why this works for the baby is pretty obvious, they get fed. This works for your wife as she gets the pleasure of knowing she is taking care of her baby's needs on a very personal one-to-one level. (It's another one of those hormone/back-to-nature things.) This works for you because—quite simply—you don't have breasts. So when your baby wakes up hungry at 2 a.m, 4 a.m., and so on, there's not a lot you can do about it. So if you like your sleep, it's best to encourage your wife to breast-feed for as long as possible.

You can also look at this time of life as your chance to watch all those TV shows you like but your wife doesn't. You know, the ones with violence and bikinis and such. Your wife will be so busy taking care of the baby she won't even have time to think about complaining about what you are watching.

Finally, you should remember that this "just-had-a-baby stage" won't last too long—a few years tops. Before you know it, you and your wife will be a team again. After all, you're going to have to pool your resources to handle everything adolescence is going to throw at you.

Handy Saying Chart

The following is a guide you can carry with you so you always know the right thing to say—or not.

Don't Say	Do Say
Man, your feet look like elephant's.	Would you like a foot rub?
Yes, you're fat.	You've never looked better.
Of course I'm scared to death about having this baby.	Of course this baby will be a change in our lives. But working together we can make it a change for the better.
I'm not doing diapers!	I'll do diapers.
Lamaze class was sure stupid tonight.	Lamaze class was sure informative tonight.
I'm going out, see you when I get back.	I'm going out, what do you need?
What's for dinner?	Let's go out for dinner.

Weight Chart

If you are a very brave man, or your wife is a very good sport, you can use this table to chart your wife's weight gain. This could make a nice future conversation piece when things get boring.

Month	Weight
1	
2	
3	
4	
5	
6	
7	
8	
9	

Okay, this was a test. If you actually considered using this chart, go back and re-read this book!

Handy definitions

Throughout your wife's pregnancy you are bound to hear countless words of pregnancy jargon. Here is a handy guide to what those words mean.

First trimester: when your wife doesn't look pregnant, but acts pregnant.

Second trimester: when your wife looks pregnant, but doesn't really act pregnant.

Third trimester: when your wife really looks pregnant, and REALLY acts pregnant. Fear her.

Afterbirth: kind of looks like the blob.

Amniocentesis: something you should be glad you never have to go through.

Amniotic sac: kind of like a really flexible football padding that covers the entire unborn baby.

Apgar score: the first of thousands of standardized tests your baby will take throughout his or her life.

Beer: something that, when consumed in large quantities, often leads to pregnancy.

Birth canal: chances are you're pretty familiar with this already.

Birthing room: a room in a hospital made to look like it's not a room in the hospital but a room in your house (especially if you keep forceps around the house). This way you'll feel more comfortable and they can charge more.

Braxton Hicks contractions: a warm up for the real thing—kind of like the pre-game show.

Breach baby: butt first.

Breasts: what you and the baby will be competing over for a while.

Cervix: chances are if you are reading this book you already know this one.

Cesarean birth: just be glad you're a man.

Colostrum: it looks kind of gross, but never tell your wife this.

Contractions: the things that hurt.

Craving: really, really, longing to eat something that seems really, really, bizarre to a non-pregnant person.

Crib: the thing you'll be spending most of your nights awake beside.

Death threats: you may get a couple of these from your wife through the course of labor. Don't sweat it though; very few wives follow up on these threats.

Delivery: what the doctor will charge you for.

Delivery room: what the hospital will charge you for.

Diaper: a cloth or plastic-like object that you will grow all too accustomed to.

Dilation: the cervix is normally closed, which is a good thing—except when the baby needs to come out. Then the cervix needs to dilate, or, in less technical terms, spread apart or slowly expand so a baby can fit through it.

Due date: the one date you can be pretty certain your baby won't arrive on.

Fainting: what happens if you look too closely at the right place at the wrong time.

Football: something that, when watched in large enough quantities, often prevents pregnancies. Actually, it often even prevents attempts at pregnancies.

Gynecologist: a doctor who gets paid to look at things that would get you arrested if you tried to look at them.

Headache: the one symptom of pregnancy that actually continues and increases as the child is born and grows.

Hormones: chemical messengers released by the body that make you either crave the opposite sex or seem crazy to the opposite sex, depending on your point of view.

In-laws: people who will tell you everything you are doing wrong throughout this pregnancy.

Kegel exercises: special exercises for pregnant women that will help prepare them for childbirth. (Screaming at the husband is technically not considered to be a Kegel exercise.)

Knife: something your wife may talk about using over and over again on you as she experiences the joy of childbirth. I believe this is called the Bobbit syndrome.

Labor: pain.

Lamaze classes: classes where you go to learn how to do something humans have been doing for roughly five million years without taking classes.

Medical insurance: if you don't have this, you really shouldn't be reading this book.

Morning sickness: barfing, throwing up, or tossing your cookies, and the general nausea your wife may or may not go through. If you want to relate to your wife, just think back to the morning after your first beer blast.

Mucus membrane: trust me, you don't want to know.

Nurse midwife: a nurse trained to delivery babies. Midwives have been around since babies started being born. Only now they are becoming kind of trendy making them cooler and more expensive than they used to be.

Ob/Gyn: a doctor who is both a gynecologist and an obstetrician, thereby making more money.

Obstetrician: a doctor who specializes in helping babies enter the world. If all goes well, he or she basically just catches, cuts, and charges.

Ovum: a fancy way of saying egg.

Placenta: looks a lot like the blob on TV. It usually follows the baby out of the mom—it's really funky looking.

Quickening: the first movement of the baby that the mommy can feel. Once it starts, it grows stronger and stronger until it seems there is a full-blown football game going on inside there.

Recovery room: if a pregnancy is especially tough (there are no easy pregnancies), the mom may spend some time in this room to be closely monitored while she regains her strength so when she recovers she'll be able to give you a good, thorough beating.

Rh incompatibility: a blood thing that is way beyond the scope of this book—and my knowledge.

Rooming in: a modern technique stolen from the cavemen that lets the whole family hang around while the mom goes through childbirth.

Sex: something that makes babies and that you won't be getting much of once the baby comes.

Sleep: something else you won't be getting much of once the baby comes.

Smoking: no jokes here, this (and drinking, and drugs) should be avoided at all cost by and around pregnant women.

Sperm: you probably refer to them as "your guys."

Superbowl Sunday: the day you really don't want your wife to go into labor.

Toxemia: something you don't want to deal with if at all possible.

Ultrasound: due to kind of old, but still kind of neat, technology, we can now use sound waves to create a picture of the baby while he or she is still inside the womb. This allows us to get actual baby pictures before we have an actual baby in our hands, thus allowing us to really embarrass our children in later years: "Look, this is what you looked like before you were born." Ultrasound pictures make lousy Christmas cards though.

Umbilical cord: the baby's lifeline while inside of the mommy. Some "lucky" daddies may get to cut this once the baby has made its first outside appearance.

Uterus: where the baby lives, grows, plays, and generally hangs out for nine months or so.

Vagina: the place where the whole adventure started.

Vasectomy: something your wife will threaten to perform on you throughout her labor.

Videotaping: something your wife will probably kill you for if you do anytime during the hospital stay.

Water breaking: if you are in the car when this happens, ACCELERATE!!!!

Wet nurse: a nurse who tries changing a newborn baby at the wrong time.

Womb: a nicer way of saying uterus.

Recording what makes your wife happy

Use this handy page to keep track of events or gestures that please your wife. Repeat them whenever possible.

Date	Gesture

Recording what displeases your wife

Use this handy page to record what makes your wife mad, angry, or furious. Then avoid doing these things. (Photocopy more as required.)

Date	Action to avoid

Pictorial Records

The following pages are reserved for you to paste in pictures of your wife.

My wife's first month

My wife's fourth month

My wife's ninth month (fear for me!)

Getting out of Trouble

Being a man, you're bound to eventually say something stupid that is bound to get you in trouble. Since your wife is pregnant she is going to be even less understanding and forgiving than usual. Therefore, you are really going to have to try a bit harder to overcome whatever it is you did wrong.

These handy certificates are meant to be an aid for getting you out of trouble. The certificate was meant to be as simple and yet as versatile as possible. Just fill in the blanks and use them wisely. (If you want to really personalize it you can write your wife's name on it.)

Certificate Of Love

I am sorry I messed up by

_____,

And I promise it won't happen again.

This certificate entitles you to

_____

And may be redeemed at any time by simply returning it to me.

(Not valid in states where this type of thing is prohibited.)

Certificate Of Love

I am sorry I messed up by

_____,

And I promise it won't happen again.

This certificate entitles you to

_____

And may be redeemed at any time by simply returning it to me.

(Not valid in states where this type of thing is prohibited.)

Certificate Of Love

I am sorry I messed up by

_____,

And I promise it won't happen again.
This certificate entitles you to

_____

And may be redeemed at any time by simply returning it to me.

(Not valid in states where this type of thing is prohibited.)

Certificate Of Love

I am sorry I messed up by

_____,

And I promise it won't happen again.
This certificate entitles you to

_____

And may be redeemed at any time by simply returning it to me.

(Not valid in states where this type of thing is prohibited.)

Certificate Of Love

I am sorry I messed up by

_____,

And I promise it won't happen again.
This certificate entitles you to

_____

And may be redeemed at any time by simply returning it to me.

(Not valid in states where this type of thing is prohibited.)

References

Shapiro, J. L. 1987. "The expectant father." *Psychology today*, January 36-39.

About the author

The author is a science writer and freelance humor writer who has a Master's degree in Human Behavior (and is slowly working on a Ph.D.) and who used to be an emergency medical technician. His first novel, *The Plutonium Blonde,* was published by Daw books in September 2001. He also writes a syndicated comic panel called *Working Daze* for United Media. He is qualified to write a book such as this because he survived the very experience he is writing about.